Ben Tomi

Songs of the Ring

Ben Tomi

Songs of the Ring

ISBN/EAN: 9783744766876

Printed in Europe, USA, Canada, Australia, Japan

Cover: Foto ©Lupo / pixelio.de

More available books at **www.hansebooks.com**

THE LIBRARY
OF
THE UNIVERSITY
OF CALIFORNIA
LOS ANGELES

Songs of The Ring.

By

Rabbi Ben Tomi.

The Secret of Success is Patience, Hope, and Trust in God.—The Secret of Happiness, giving Happiness to others.

NEW YORK:
PUBLISHED BY WALTER GIBSON,
59 Liberty Street.
1866.

Entered according to Act of Congress, in the year 1866, by
WALTER GIBSON,
In the Clerk's Office of the District Court of the United States for the Southern District of New York.

TO

ALL WHO WEARY AND ARE HEAVY LADEN,

THIS BOOK

IS

DEDICATED

BY

RABBI BEN TOMI.

CONTENTS.

The Secret of Happiness	9
O ye who Weary	10
The First Sabbath	11
The First New Year	12
The First Christmas	14
New Year Song	16
A Winter Day	16
Clover Hill	18
The Rabbi's Conviction	19
The Withered Tree	20
The Little Street-Sweeper	21
The Violet	24
Return of the Bluebird	25
The Weeping Willow	26
The Search for Peace	28
Perfect Peace	30
Oh, what is Life?	31
There are Moments in Life	31

Let the Silver Cord be loosed	32
Why fear, O Man?	33
The Soldier's Rest	35
The Crucifixion	38
From 7th Chapter of St. Luke	40
Charity	41
I Feel the Lord doth bless	42
"Blessed are the Poor in Spirit"	43
"Daughter, be of Good Comfort"	44
"Let not thy Left Hand know what thy Right Hand doeth"	45
"Thy Sins be Forgiven"	46
Trust and Pray	46
The Lord's Prayer	47
When I Reflect on All the Deeds	48
O ye of Little Faith	49
"Go, and Sin no more"	50
To an Iceberg at Sea	51
To a Mother, on the Death of a Child	52
"I know that my Redeemer Liveth"	53
"Trust ye in the Lord forever"	54
Jesus, Rock of my Salvation	55
"Cast thy Bread upon the Waters"	56
I thank Thee, Lord, for every Gift	57
The Wisdom of King David	58
The Victory of King Asa	59
The Prayer of King Asa	61
"Be ye Strong"	61

CONTENTS.

The Punishment of Uzziah . . .	62
From Deuteronomy 24th . . .	63
From Job 23d	64
He Feedeth on Ashes . . .	65
"To whom will ye liken God?" . .	66
From Isaiah 40th	67
From Proverbs 26th . . .	68
From Proverbs 13th . . .	69
From Isaiah 32d	70
"If ye have Faith and doubt not" . .	71
Stephen before the Council . .	72
The Preacher	74
"Remember thy Creator" . . .	76
"Boast not Thyself of to-morrow" .	77
"All Flesh is Grass"	78
"A Man that has Friends, must show himself friendly"	79
Prayer of Agur	80
Father of Mercies	81
Prayer of Habakkuk	81
Prayer of the Psalmist — Dark Clouds .	83
The Blessings of Obedience to God .	84
The Angel Child	85
The Goodness of God	86
"The Lord is my Shepherd" . . .	87
Unto the Lord give Thanks . .	88
Unless the Lord be with us . .	89
Praise God	90

I love the Lord my God	90
"They that sow in Tears"	91
"Unto Thee O Lord, do I Lift up my Soul"	92
Who is strong like the Lord?	92
Thou art my Hiding-Place, O God	93
"Commit thy Way unto the Lord"	94
Help cometh from the Lord	94
"Whom have I in Heaven but Thee?"	95
The mighty Power of God	97
A Prayer — Part 1. The Answer — Part 2	98
In Memoriam	99

SONGS OF THE RING.

THE SECRET OF HAPPINESS.

The words of the Rabbi Ben Tomi,
   The words which now I sing,
Are engraved in mystic signs
   On the Rabbi's sacred ring.

My son! dost thou wish to know
   The secret of worldly success?
And having that knowledge, learn
   The secret of happiness?

Remember, thou art but man,
   Formed out of crumbling dust;
Then learn in patience to wait,
   To hope, and in God to trust.

From Patience, Experience comes,
   From Experience, Hope we possess;
And he who will trust in his God,
   His God will assuredly bless.

Then scatter thy bounties abroad
   To less fortunate sisters and brothers,
For happiness only is found
   By giving it unto others.

OH, YE WHO WEARY.

Oh, ye who weary and are sad,
   Who heavy laden be,
Ask if your burden heavier is
   Than others you may see.

The weight of it may bear you down
   With tiresome toil and heat,
But in your travail you may fall
   And clasp a Saviour's feet.

The Saviour who in patience bore
   A burden heavier still,
The cross which bowed him to the earth,
   Ascending Calvary's Hill.

The Saviour who in mercy gave
   This burden unto you,
Which by its weight your soul may save,
   And give you life anew.

THE FIRST SABBATH.

GENESIS, CHAPTER II.

This is the holy Sabbath day,
    The day our God has blest,
Created, sanctified by Him
    To be a day of rest.

The heavens and all the earth complete,
    Jehovah resting stood,
And seeing all that He had made,
    Pronounced it very good.

All nature joyous at its birth,
    The voice of Heaven had heard,
And bowed in holy reverence
    Before the mighty word.

The light shone softer on that day,
    Obedient to God's will;
In Eden, bird and beast reposed,
    And everything was still.

The morning stars together sang
    A song which filled the sky;
And all the sons of God did shout
    Praise to the Lord Most High.

While angels, round the throne of God,
    Proclaimed with joyous zest
The last day sanctified by love,
    The brightest and the best.

THE FIRST NEW YEAR.

In chaos all was black as night,
God spake the word, "Let there be light:"
    And light shone far and near;
Bright angels present at the birth,
Sang anthems to the new-born earth,
    And hailed the first new year.

The infant Sun, his natal day,
Shot boldly forth a loving ray
    Upon a barren clod,
Which, overjoyed with unknown bliss,
In glad response to Heaven's first kiss,
    Bore fruits and flowers to God.

The crescent Moon, the lesser light,
Cast through the spangled veil of night
    Her glance upon the deep;
And falling on a wild wave's crest,
So calmed and lulled it into rest,
    It rocked itself to sleep.

Five thousand years and more have flown
Since first upon a new year shone
    The Sun which shines to-day;
Five thousand years with changes fraught,
To him no change or rest have brought,
    Or dimmed one quenchless ray.

Five thousand years, and more, have fled
Since first the new-year young moon shed
    Her light upon the sea ;
Five thousand years the sea has sighed,
Five thousand years the ebb and tide
    Have answered her decree.

In Eden, when the day's last gleam
Was falling soft on wood and stream,
    The voice of God was heard ;
While man, the creature of his hand,
In pristine purity would stand
    And listen to the word.

Five thousand years, and more, have sped
Since first Jehovah deigned to tread
    On Eden's sacred sod, —
Five thousand years of sad remorse,
For Eve and Adam's sinful course,
    In disobeying God.

The God, who, for five thousand years,
Has heard the prayers and dried the tears
    Of sorrow-stricken men ;
The God who Adam's seed to save,
His only son a victim gave,
    Is now the same as then.

Five thousand years on which were cast
So many doubts, are now the past,
    And teach man not to fear ;
But trust unto the God who said,
"Let there be light," and light obeyed,
    And welcome each new year.

With stern resolve to do God's will,
Under affliction to be still,
   Believing all for best;
So when this new year, like the last,
Shall be entombèd in the past,
   We all can call it blest.

THE FIRST CHRISTMAS.

ST. LUKE.

In Bethlehem, round a stable rude,
In holy, reverent attitude,
   A host of angels hover,
To welcome to a lowly manger
The King of kings, a pilgrim stranger,
   Who came our sins to cover.

No fiery sun of garish day
Illumed the stable where he lay,
   Or flickered on his sight;
The glory of himself shone out,
And lit the stable round about, —
   Of all the world the light.

His star from fixedness released,
To homage pay came from the east,
   And stood o'er Bethlehem's sod,
While Magi following, Heaven foretold,
Unto the child brought gifts of gold,
   And worshipped him, their God.

The shepherds, keeping watch by night,
Are overpowered by unknown light
   Of glory shining round;
And feeling that the Lord is near,
Are filled with supernatural fear,
   And kneel upon the ground, —

When lo! an angel from whom shone
The glory of the Father's throne,
   Said, Be ye not afraid!
And in a soft, angelic voice,
Spake tidings good, and said, Rejoice,
   Be all your doubts allayed;

For unto you is born this day,
And in a manger now doth lay
   A Saviour, Christ the Lord;
In earth henceforth there shall be peace,
His acts of love shall never cease,
   He is the Son of God!

While seraphs of the heavenly host,
To Father, Son, and Holy Ghost,
   Sang glory! glory! glory!
And every cherub voice on high,
Did echo through the azure sky
   So wonderful a story.

NEW YEAR SONG.

I THANK thee, Lord, that thou hast led
    Thy servant through this year,
And start a new one now to tread,
    Without one doubt or fear,
Remembering that I am but dust,
And living, Lord, in hope and trust.

With firm, relying trust I cast
    My burdens, Lord, on thee ;
Thy tender mercies in the past
    Give future hope to me,
That thou by him wilt ever stand,
Whom thou hast holden by the hand.

A WINTER DAY.

THE snow lies on the ground,
    The trees are stripped and bare,
And the sunbeam chilly nipped
    By the hazy, murky air.

The black crow gloomy sits
    With her head beneath her wing,
In her sable feathers wrapped
    Like a mourner for the spring.

The cedar and the laurel,
   Defiant of the blast,
Stand in glory ever green
   Like the memory of the past.

The wind sighs through the oak
   With a sad and mournful strain,
Which the cedar echoes back, —
   That spring will come again.

That though the leaves, her children,
   Are lying dead around,
They are keeping warm the sap
   Of their mother in the ground.

The little Quaker snowbird,
   Deprived of grain for food,
Plucks the tasteless crimson berry,
   And feels that God is good.

Then in some rocky crevice
   Hides from tempest and the rain,
For the God of nature tells him
   That the sun will shine again.

The squirrel dormant lies
   In his nut-encircled nest,
And clasps his cherished partner
   With a chip-chip to his breast.

The waterfall hangs silent,
   A glittering sheet of ice,
Like crystals in a cavern,
   Of strange and wild device.

The trout in crystal bower
 Doth still and torpid lay,
Dreaming of the noisy ripple
 Which he heard in sunny May.

Not a murmur can we hear
 From these children of the wood,
For they know their mother Nature
 Sends the winter for their good.

Then let me learn from nature
 To bear God's holy will,
And to quell my thoughts insurgent,
 With His saying, "Peace, be still."

CLOVER HILL.

By a little stream which rippled
 Through the valley and the wood,
Dwelt an old man and his wife,
 Both gentle, kind, and good.

They never turned their faces
 From the suffering and the poor,
And the pilgrim and the stranger
 Met a welcome at their door.

They bore their burdens meekly,
 And did their Master's will,
And thought all things were for the best,
 In their home at Clover Hill.

And when life's journey ended,
  They laid them down to sleep,
Where the violets grow above them
  And the willows o'er them weep.

THE RABBI'S CONVICTION.

The Rabbi Ben Tomi was poor,
  He knew that gold was a curse;
He left open the latch of his door,
  And gave away all in his purse.

For each piece of silver he gave,
  He found a gold coin in its place;
He grew rich and determined to save,
  And his wealth and his meanness kept pace.

He fastened the latch of his door,
  On his money-bags nightly would kneel;
Thought that none but the wicked were poor,
  Nor cared if they starved or should steal.

But the Lord, in his mercy, looked down
  On the Rabbi Ben Tomi one day;
On his avarice sternly did frown,
  And took half of his riches away.

And the Rabbi awoke to the thought,
  If this money had only been given,
His work would have not gone for nought,
  But be credited to him in heaven.

So he bowed to the loss and did say,
    I see it is useless to hoard,
It is the Lord giveth and taketh away;
    Bless'd be the name of the Lord.

And he put out his latch-string with love,
    Gave freely in hope and in trust,
And invested his treasures above,
    Where neither is moth nor is rust.

Then the Lord, in his mercy, did smile,
    And all of his gifts did increase,
And Ben Tomi grew rich all the while,
    And his days and nights ended in peace.

THE WITHERED TREE.

Old withered tree, beneath thy shade
In infancy I oft have played,
And from thy branches often heard
The loving song of summer bird.

But thou and I are both grown old,
Our day has passed, our tale been told,
And thou who hast a century stood,
Art fit alone for kindling-wood.

But in thy old and glorious age,
My sorrow still thou canst assuage;
Thou who hast sheltered me from storm,
Can now console and keep me warm.

And when upon my hearth I place
Thy withered trunk, then I will trace,
In every flame that leaps on high,
Some youthful hopes which withered lie,

And grow each hour more melancholy
To watch thy embers dying slowly;
And think, that, as the old log crashes,
Both of our lives must end in ashes.

Though still to thee my heart shall yearn,
Thy ashes shall adorn no urn,
But, better far, shall lightly rest
Upon the earth, thy mother's breast,

And so enrich the soil around,
That fruits and flowers will there abound,
And man upon the spot shall gaze
With eye entranced and with amaze.

Then I will say, Oh, stranger, see
My monument to the withered tree.

THE LITTLE STREET-SWEEPER.

"SUFFER LITTLE CHILDREN TO COME UNTO ME."

  CLAD in rags,
   Tattered and torn,
  Hatless and shoeless,
   Sad and forlorn,

Cheerless and dreary
  She sweeps the street,
Now here, now there,
  Beneath horses' feet;
Running her race
  From cradle to tomb,
Turning and twisting
  Her worn-out broom.

Pause and gaze
  As you pass her by,
Thin, pale face
  And sunken eye;
Quick in motion,
  Expression wild,
Infantile shape,
  A senile child.
Pity her sad
  And lonely condition,
Toss her a penny,
  Her height of ambition.

What has she done
  That her fate should be so
Filled up with misery,
  Sorrow, and woe?
What did she do
  To inherit such doom, —
Birth, in a cellar,
  Fortune, a broom?

Who was her mother?
  No one can tell;
Like Eve she was tempted,
  Like Eve she fell.

Who was her father?
  God only knows;
He in his time
  The truth will disclose.

Say, is she human
  Flesh and bones,
Or grown like the grass
  From between the stones?

Oh! she is human,
  Food for the grave,
Born of a woman,
  A soul to save.
Do not despise her,
  A trifle give;
Like you she is struggling
  Only to live.

She is no mendicant;
  See her now,
Earning her bread
  By the sweat of her brow.
Had she been reared
  In luxury's lap,
Instead of offal,
  Nurtured on pap;
Had she been taught
  God's Holy Word,
Instead of the oaths
  She ever has heard;
She might have been
  Of the chosen few,
And a great deal better
  Than I or you.

She is a sister
  Of crumbling dust.
Give of your loaf,
  She wants but a crust.

Pity her sad
  And lonely condition,
Give her a penny,
  Her height of ambition;
And the Child Lover
  Your action will see
Who said suffer children
  To come unto me.
As you have given
  To this lonely one,
Your gift be recorded
  As unto God done.

THE VIOLET.

Spake the violet to herself,
  When she felt the warmth of spring,
"What fond memory of the past
  Doth a ray of sunshine bring.

"I have slumbered all the winter,
  In a dark and frozen clod,
Nor have thought, until to-day,
  Of appealing to my God.

"I will burst the earthen fetters
  Which have held me in their thrall,
And will feel my way to sunshine,
  As I on and upward crawl."

Then a little shoot sprung forth,
  And did on and upward creep,
And while struggling for the sunshine,
  Nor wearied nor did sleep.

But found itself, one morning,
  On the holiest of the seven,
In the glory of the sunshine,
  And gazing up to heaven;

When it grew and flourished bravely,
  Watched by mercy and by power,
And in thankfulness to heaven,
  Bloomed a fair and lovely flower.

RETURN OF THE BLUEBIRD.

A BLUEBIRD, from the Sunny South,
  Flew North on hurried wing,
To be the first to welcome back,
  With song, the coming spring.

No blade of grass, no leaf he saw,
  No hopeful olive-branch,
To keep his heart, like Noah's dove,
  In purpose, true and staunch.

But on a gnarled and leafless tree
　He hopped and twittered long,
And waited for some budding sign,
　To tune his voice to song.

When lo! he downward cast his eyes
　Upon the teeming sod,
And saw one tender, struggling plant,
　Which raised itself to God.

Then loud and sweet the warbled song,
　The little wanderer woke,
To let all nature know the sleep
　Of nature had been broke.

THE WEEPING WILLOW.

Weeping willow,
　Why dost thou weep?
Is it over the dead
　Who beneath thee sleep?
Or is it that thou
　Hast lived so long,
As to know the world
　And to see the wrong
Done, day by day,
　By all who can
Take something away
　From his fellow man?

Weeping willow,
　Bending, weeping,
While I gaze on thee
　My flesh is creeping.
Each gentle breeze,
　As it passes by,
Like Æolian harps,
　Through thy branches sigh, —
Not in a harsh,
　Discordant tone,
But with low and plaintive
　And tender moan,
As though it mourned
　Some memory past,
And each sound given
　Might be the last.

Oh! thou art a sad
　And sorrowful tree,
Companion unfit
　For a man like me.
I do not wish
　To have thee near,
With thy crouching shape
　And quivering fear;
I love far more
　The brave old oak,
That defies the blast
　And the lightning-stroke;
That rears his head
　Aloft on high,
Nor tells his fear
　With quivering sigh,

But sturdily meets,
  Like the son of giants,
The fiercest storm,
  With stern defiance.

Oh, weeping willow,
  Thy fate is hard,
By nature made
  For the dim churchyard,
Where thy yielding twigs
  May sadly wave
Over each old
  And new-made grave.
Then wave thou there,
  And moan and weep
Over the dead
  Who beneath thee sleep.

THE SEARCH FOR PEACE.

THE Rabbi Ben Tomi sought for peace,
  And determined he would dwell
Afar from the world, at Clover Hill,
  In a hermit's quiet cell; —

Afar from the noise and din of town,
  From ambition, pride, and strife,
Where alone in peace he could sit him down,
  To fight the battle of life.

But he found that the pulse of man still beat,
  That from thought there was no release,
And the pining he felt for the world he left,
  Taught solitude was not peace.

Then to stream and field he bade farewell,
  And the angel sought to meet,
No longer in woods and flowery dell,
  But in walks of crowded street.

He wandered and sauntered and strolled along,
Through the gay and laughing and joyous throng,
  But found no peace was there;
For he read with clear and searching eye,
In the mocking smile of passers-by,
  The skeleton lines of care.

Then he paused and spake to a weary child,
  Who the crossing swept and cleaned,
And asked why at mirth she never smiled,
  And why on her broom she leaned;
And he found that from her all hope had fled,
She toiled all day, but she wanted bread.

Then he brought to that wan and weary face
  A smile which was fair to see,
As a purse in her hand he kindly placed,
  A genuine charity.
And the Rabbi Ben Tomi his search did cease,
For he found that in charity there was peace.

PERFECT PEACE.

There is a peace which far exceeds
    All joys the world can give ;
Which by its perfect stillness leads
    The soul in hope to live.

A peace which falls on throbbing breast,
    Accepting what may be,
And lulls each troubled wave to rest,
    Like moonlight on the sea.

A peace, which, when dark clouds shall roll
    Along life's weary way,
Can shed a light upon the soul,
    And teach us how to pray.

A peace which tells us, though our prayer
    Be said with parting breath,
We still are objects of God's care,
    And triumphs over death.

That peace, each day that I shall live,
    I ask on bended knee,
In love and mercy thou wilt give,
    O Lord, my God, to me.

OH, WHAT IS LIFE?

Oh, what is life, that I should wish
  To linger longer here,
Where every day is filled with doubt,
  And every night with fear?

Where, though a man be born a king,
  Or live an abject slave,
He treads a sure and beaten path,
  Which leads him to the grave.

While every moment that he spends,
  Preparing here to stay,
Unfits him for the coming time,
  When he must go away.

Then learn, O man, to look to death,
  Which ends this mortal strife,
Not as a final foe to dread,
  But as the birth of life.

THERE ARE MOMENTS IN LIFE.

There are moments in life so fearfully dark,
  So full of grief and sorrow,
That like a mariner, tempest-tossed,
  Who clings to a sinking, shipwrecked bark,
And feels that all of his hope is lost, —
  We dread to see to-morrow.

But far as the straining eye can reach,
    Where the clouds and wild waves meet,
A glimmering light, through the murky night,
    Shows a lighthouse upon the beach,
And the fainting swimmer still struggles on,
With a ray of hope in his heart forlorn.

So we, when we faint upon our way,
    And feel that the world is dross,
Have only to raise our downcast eyes,
    And fix them upon the cross,
At the foot of which, though trouble-stranded,
We may rest in peace, by mercy landed.

When the lighthouse Keeper will hear our cry,
    Shrill rising above the wind,
And wrapped in the mantle of charity,
    Which he wears for all mankind ;
By the waves of trouble washed from sin,
To the haven of rest will take us in.

LET THE SILVER CORD BE LOOSED.

Let the silver cord be loosed,
    Let the golden bowl be broke,
For I weary of this world,
    And I suffer from its yoke.
My life is nought but vanity,
    Wherever I may roam.
Father of mercies, hear my prayer,
    And take me to thy home.

My days are full of sorrow,
   My nights are full of grief,
I dread to see the morrow,
   For it brings me no relief.
And I see that all is vanity
   Wherever I may roam;
Father of mercies, hear my prayer,
   And take me to thy home.

The wild beast has his lair,
   The eagle has his nest,
But man has not a dwelling-place
   Where he can safely rest.
Then end my earthly pilgrimage,
   Let me no longer roam,
But take me, Father, to thyself,
   And keep me in thy home.

Thy home, the heaven of heavens,
   Where joy eternal reigns,
Where saint and seraphim exalt
   Thy love in heavenly strains;
Thy home, where I shall ever dwell
   With the perfect and the blest,
Where the wicked cease from troubling,
   And the weary are at rest.

WHY FEAR, O MAN?

Why fear, O man, though dark the path,
   And clouds above thee lower,
The tempest and the storm are but
   The shadow of God's power,

Which oftentimes he casts before
    His footsteps, from above,
That when dispelled, the frighted soul
    May feel his power is love.

The marble block, when chipped and torn
    Beneath the sculptor's hand,
From being shapeless and forlorn,
    An angel form doth stand,

Which with a shout of joy would praise
    The arm which hammered well,
And by his strength and power had wrought
    So wonderful a spell.

The flower to which the winter blast
    Long days of darkness bring,
Beneath the mantle of the snow,
    Is cherished for the spring.

The stream whose constant rippling song
    Is stilled by icy thrall,
And hanging stiff in glittering spars
    Around the waterfall,

Beneath God's warm and loving sun,
    From frozen sleep awakes,
And to its love, the deep blue sea,
    A fuller offering takes.

Then learn from nature, patiently,
    Whate'er thy lot, to bear,
Believing, trusting all to God,
    And his protecting care.

So when thy soul shall leave the flesh,
  A miserable clod,
Thy spirit, purified by faith,
  Shall wing its way to God.

THE SOLDIER'S REST.

On a blood-stained field
  A soldier lay,
He had fought his fight,
  He had won the day.

The crinkling snow
  Was red with blood,
And purple ran
  The river's flood,

While through the trees
  The wind was sighing
A mournful requiem
  O'er the dying.

He heard no shout
  Of victory swell
On the mountain steep
  Or the snow-clad dell,

For his heart was far
  From the battle-strife,
And nestled home
  With his child and wife.

When he closed his eyes,
  He saw one there,
With the chubby hands,
  And the curly hair,

And the loving eyes
  Which smiled on him,
While his were closing,
  Glazed and dim.

And he knew that the sun
  Would set that day,
On a darkened hearth
  And a lump of clay.

With his fingers, black
  From the smoke and flame,
Wet with the blood
  Which from him came,

He brushed the tear
  From his trembling eye,
Which trickling fell,
  As his hour drew nigh.

The eye of the past
  In his heart did stare;
He thought of his mother,
  His infant prayer;

Of now that I lay me
  Adown to sleep,
I pray that the Lord
  My soul will keep;

Of our Father who art
    And ever will be,
As he used to say
    At his mother's knee;

Of Jesus the Saviour,
    Of God the Son,
Who, dying, cried out,
    "Thy will be done."

And as weaker he grew
    In the chilling air,
The faster his lips
    Did move in prayer,

Till all things earthly
    Became as dross,
And he saw in the clouds
    A simple cross

Which rose above
    Like a pillar of fire,
And led him to look
    Still higher and higher,

Till he saw the bow
    Of promise there,
And he knew that God
    Had heard his prayer.

And he sank to sleep
    On a Saviour's breast,
With the words, "I have found
    The soldier's rest."

THE CRUCIFIXION.

See the Saviour of mankind,
    From the hall of Pilate led;
See the crown of plaited thorns,
    Twisted round his holy head.

See him climb the rugged steep,
    Burdened with his dreadful cross;
Tears of sorrow he doth weep,
    Not at his, but at man's loss.

See the scourges on his back,
    See the harsh, relentless goad,
Urging on his quivering frame,
    As it faints beneath his load.

See the mockers and the scoffers
    As around his cross they stand;
See the agony he suffers,
    See the nail-prints in his hand.

Hear him pray unto his Father,
    With his lips of bloodless hue, —
"Father! Father! oh, forgive them,
    For they know not what they do."

See him hiding all his power,
    Power of vengeance, power to kill,
Meekly bearing all his sorrow,
    Yielding to his Father's will.

See the sadness and the sorrow,
    Falling o'er the heavenly host,
When the Lamb cries, "It is finished,"
    Bows his head, yields up the ghost.

Hear the mournful, plaintive echo,
    Through the mansions of the sky,
As the angels bear his spirit
    To his Father's throne on high.

See the sun his outraged presence
    Hide beneath a veil of gloom,
As though nature dare not witness
    To the God of nature's doom.

Feel the earth with terror quaking,
    See the graves give up the dead,
Hear his cry unto his Father,
    When a Saviour's spirit fled.

Fled from out his flesh of suffering,
    To eternal thrones on high,
Whence he'll come in power and glory,
    God, the judge of you and I.

You and I, who, by our actions,
    Daily done while in the flesh,
Show him that he suffered vainly,
    Crucify the Lord afresh.

See the crucifiers shrinking,
    Filled with fear and sharp remorse,
Leaving him, their King and Saviour,
    Hanging dead upon the cross.

On the cross thenceforth forever
  Made the means of pardoning grace;
On the cross thenceforth forever
  Stamped upon each guilty face.

Let me, like the worn centurion,
  Gazing through the fleshly clod,
Seeing but thy mighty spirit,
  Feel this was the Son of God.

Give me faith and trust, O Jesus,
  God incarnate, Three in One,
Flying to thy cross for refuge,
  Let thy will, not mine, be done.

Let thy cross my fainting spirit
  Cheer, whene'er my heart grows sadder;
Let it be, O Lord, to me,
  Like the patriarch Jacob's ladder.

Let the base be firmly planted
  On Mount Calvary's sacred sod,
And the topmost round be resting
  On the mercy of my God.

FROM THE SEVENTH CHAPTER OF ST. LUKE.

When she who at our Saviour's feet
  Her tears repentant shed,
And loving much, did wipe them with
  The soft hair of her head;

The Pharisee did murmur loud,
  That such a sinner dare,
Without reproof, to humbly kneel
  In penitential prayer.

But He who is the sinner's friend,
  Gazed on with glad emotion,
And let her clasp his sacred feet
  With sorrowful devotion.

And spake the words which oft have healed
  The bruised and breaking heart,
And caused the light of happier days
  In memory to start.

To whom so little is forgiven,
  They never can adore,
Like one whose sins so many were,
  Yet still whose love was more.

For this one act of faith and love
  Her sins were all forgiven,
And saved by faith, she went in peace,
  And rests with him in heaven.

CHARITY.

1 Corinthians, Chap. XIII.

Though I should speak as angels speak,
  No use my words would be,
If in my heart I am unkind,
  And have not charity.

The charity which suffereth long,
　　Is kind and envieth not;
The charity in which a wrong
　　Is patiently forgot.

The charity which beareth all,
　　Believes, hopes, and endures,
And when I faint upon my way,
　　My weakness promptly cures.

The simple words of man shall cease,
　　And knowledge pass away,
The voice of prophecy be still,
　　But charity will stay.

And now, faith, hope, and charity
　　Abide, but of the three,
Though all are great, the greatest gem
　　Of these is charity.

I FEEL THE LORD DOTH BLESS.

In my worldly success
　　My soul is full of fear,
I feel the Lord doth bless,
　　That his spirit is near.
God of omnipotence,
　　Incarnate Three in One,
My prayer shall ever be,
　　Thy holy will be done.

Oh, soul, while thou livest,
   Let the Lord be thy stay,
It is the Lord giveth,
   And who taketh away.
In joy or in sorrow,
   Love and fear him the same;
Blessed forever be
   The Lord's holy name.

BLESSED ARE THE POOR IN SPIRIT.

MATTHEW, CHAPTER V.

BLESS'D are all the poor in spirit,
   Bless'd are all the meek,
Bless'd are all who righteousness
   Shall hunger for and seek.

Bless'd are all the merciful,
   They mercy shall obtain,
And when they cry unto the Lord,
   They shall not cry in vain.

Bless'd are all the pure in heart,
   For when their path is trod,
The Father's kingdom shall be theirs,
   And they shall see their God.

DAUGHTER, BE OF GOOD COMFORT.

MATTHEW, CHAPTER IX.

A woman who had suffered long,
  With sickness none could cure,
Close to the feet of Jesus came,
  And touched his garment pure;

For she had said within herself,
  "Would I this pain dispel,
Let me but touch his garment's hem,
  And I'll be whole and well."

When Jesus turned around and saw
  The faith within her soul,
He said, "Good comfort be to thee,
  Thy faith has made thee whole."

And she who humbly trusted to
  God's mercy, love, and power,
In her humility and faith,
  Was made whole from that hour.

"LET NOT THY LEFT HAND KNOW WHAT THY RIGHT HAND DOETH."

MATTHEW, CHAPTER VI.

Give unto him that asketh thee,
  Turn not thy face away,
Lest he who gave us this command,
  Should heed not when ye pray.

And take ye heed ye do not give
  Your alms for men to see,
Or God will give you no reward, —
  It is not charity.

But when thou doest any alms,
  To do it be not slow,
And what thy right hand doeth oft,
  Thy left hand should not know.

Then He who sees thy secret heart,
  Thy Father and the Son,
Will openly reward the deeds
  Thou secretly hast done.

"THY SINS BE FORGIVEN."

MATTHEW, CHAPTER IX.

To him who sick of palsy lay
    In suffering on his bed,
These words of comfort for his faith,
    Our blessed Saviour said:

" Faint not, O son, be of good cheer,
    Thy sins forgiven be;
Arise! take up thy bed and walk,
    That all the world may see."

And he arose and went his way,
    A well man from that hour,
And they who saw, did worship God,
    And glorify his power.

TRUST AND PRAY.

When servants of the living God
    Were in the furnace tried,
The God in whom they put their trust,
    Was walking by their side.

When to the banks of Cherith Brook
　　The good Elijah fled,
God sent the ravens, night and morn,
　　To bring him flesh and bread.

When in the Shunam's darkened house
　　Elisha knelt in prayer,
And humbly asked the Lord of Hosts
　　The Shunam's child to spare,

The God of heaven in pity gazed
　　Upon the Shunam's wife,
And gave Elisha power to call
　　The dead child back to life.

God is the same to-day as then,
　　And will extend his care
To all who put their trust in him,
　　And call on him in prayer.

THE LORD'S PRAYER.

Our Father, who art in heaven,
　　Hallowed be thy name.
Thy kingdom come, thy will be done
　　In heaven and earth the same.

Give us this day our daily bread,
　　Our trespasses forgive,
As we forgive the trespasses
　　Of those with whom we live.

And keep us from temptation, Lord,
  From evil us deliver,
For thine the kingdom, power is,
  And glory be forever.

WHEN I REFLECT ON ALL THE DEEDS.

When I reflect on all the deeds
  The Lord has done for me,
His lowly birth and suffering,
  His death upon the tree;
I tremble at the awful love
To man below from God above.

The God who, when he chastens me,
  Hears murmuring at my lot;
The God who, when he blesses me,
  Is impiously forgot;
The God who, in a moment's wrath,
Can sweep the worm from out his path.

Oh, what am I that I should dare,
  While grovelling in the dust,
To doubt God's wisdom or his care,
  Or falter in my trust?
Can earthly force resist God's power,
Or add to human life one hour?

Wherefore in ashes I repent,
  And by myself abhorred,
Will think all things are for the best,
  And trust unto the Lord.
His every act, like Job, I'll praise,
That he may bless my latter days.

"O YE OF LITTLE FAITH."

O YE of little faith, who wish
    That ye had ne'er been born,
And in your murmuring reject
    The gifts of God with scorn;

Behold the lily of the field,
    The wild fowl of the air,
How each gives evidence to man,
    Of God's paternal care.

How can you see the glorious sun
    In golden splendor rise,
And not thank God, in gratitude,
    That ye were born with eyes?

How can you listen to the bird
    Which warbles in the tree,
And not thank God that ye have ears
    To hear his melody?

How can you speak in pity to
    The dumb, the halt, and lame,
And not thank God that, in his wrath,
    He made you not the same?

The God of God, the Light of Light,
    Creator by a breath,
Who covered all his glory with
    The gloomy pall of death.

The God by whom all things were made,
    Yet counted it no loss
To be laid in a manger,
    And die upon the cross,

That he might show to sinful man,
    The hopeless and forlorn,
That in the future there was life
    To all who had been born.

"GO, AND SIN NO MORE."

John, Chapter VIII.

When she who had been found in sin,
    Before the Lord was brought,
He stooped and wrote upon the sand,
    As though he heard not aught;

And showed to men that although sin
    Might be as clear as day,
Like traces marked upon the sand,
    It could be washed away.

So when again they told their tale,
    He spoke in gentle tone, —
"Let him who is without a sin
    First cast at her a stone."

And they which heard, by conscience struck,
    Dared not to raise a stone,
But all went out and left the Lord,
    With her who sinned, alone.

Then spake the Lord, "Where have they gone,
  They who accused before?
They do not now condemn, nor I,
  Go, thou, and sin no more."

TO AN ICEBERG.

BEAUTIFUL iceberg, pure and cold,
Floating along so graceful and bold,
Messenger from some unknown sea,
Hurrying to eternity.

Formed far off in the polar zone,
Where the footstep of man is yet unknown,
Spray from the ocean dashed to land,
Fettered by Winter's strong, icy hand.

Essence of purity, covered with snow,
A thing too pure for this world of woe,
Bearing aloft so proud a crest,
On which tarnish or stain can never rest.

Oh, why can the soul of man not be
As pure as this gem from the frozen sea,
Free from all sorrow, sin, and malice,
Cased by God in a crystal palace?

Fostered in youth by a father's care,
Guarded through life by a mother's prayer,
Still he is cursed with the brand of sin,
False to his duty and hollow within.

Essence of purity ! nought so pure
In this world of ours can ever endure,
And before your course seems half-way run,
You will shrink and melt 'neath the summer sun.

TO A MOTHER, ON THE DEATH OF HER CHILD.

The shaft of death has struck its mark,
   Thy infant has been taken,
But trust thou in a Saviour's love,
   Thou shalt not be forsaken.

To bear thy early loss,
   He strength to thee will give;
Remember that upon the cross
   He died that she might live.

From sin and sorrow free,
   Her spirit is at rest,
And gently nestles now to sleep,
   Safe in a Saviour's breast.

Then weep no more for one
   For whom to weep is vain;
Although it is thy earthly loss,
   It is her heavenly gain.

"I KNOW THAT MY REDEEMER LIVETH."

JOB, CHAPTER XIX.

When all familiar friends have failed,
   And none a kind word gives,
I do not faint, for well I know
   That my Redeemer lives.

That at the latter day he'll stand
   Himself upon the earth,
To judge of all the deeds I've done,
   E'en from my earliest birth.

Although with worms this form shall lie,
   Beneath the grass-grown sod,
Yet in my flesh it promised is
   That I shall see my God.

That he will read this heart aright,
   Though sinful it may be,
And cleanse it with his precious blood
   Which he has shed for me.

Then what to me can be the frown
   Which worldly hatred gives,
When I the blessed promise have,
   That my Redeemer lives.

"TRUST YE IN THE LORD FOREVER."

Isaiah, Chapter XXVI, Vs. 3, 4.

In perfect peace thou wilt him keep
   Whose mind on thee is stayed,
Because his trust is placed in thee,
Jehovah, Lord of earth and sea,
   And all that has been made.

Then trust ye ever in the Lord,
   This promise doth he give,
Though earthly sorrows may be sent,
Meekly to bear them with content,
   And ye shall ever live.

A shadow on your life may fall
   And fill you with despair,
But trust ye in the Lord of all,
He answers to the humblest call
   Of one who kneels in prayer.

Then trust ye ever in the Lord,
   Trust as the saints of old;
With peace of mind ye shall be blest,
Believing all is for the best,
   Till ye the end behold.

"JESUS, ROCK OF MY SALVATION."

Jesus, rock of my salvation,
    Let me anchor fast to thee,
Lest my bark of hope should founder
    In life's dark, tempestuous sea;
Faith and trust in me still cherish
Save me, Lord, or I shall perish.

Thou! my rock of strength and refuge,
    On thy mercy I rely,
Thou, a man of many sorrows,
    Listen to my helpless cry;
Faith and trust in me still cherish,
Save me, Lord, or I shall perish.

Thou! who, walking on the water,
    Bad'st thy servant come to thee,
Stretching out thy hand to save him,
    When he sank beneath the sea;
Faith and trust in me still cherish,
Save me, Lord, or I shall perish.

Thou! who like a human brother
    Weeping over Lazarus' doom,
By thy mighty power didst call him
    From his dark and silent tomb;
Faith and trust in me still cherish,
Save me, Lord, or I shall perish.

Thou! who sick and lame didst heal,
    Sight unto the blind didst give,
Suffering on the shameful cross
    That the son of man might live;
Faith and trust in me still cherish,
Save me, Lord, or I shall perish.

Thou! who through the vale of death
    Patiently thy way hast trod,
When I cross the shadowy river,
    Be thou near me, Son of God;
Faith and trust in me still cherish,
Save me, Lord, or I shall perish.

"CAST THY BREAD UPON THE WATERS."

ECCLESIASTES XI.

Cast thy bread upon the waters,
    It will return to thee,
Of charity there is no crumb
    Jehovah does not see.

Fear not, O blind and selfish man,
    Thy bread will not return,
Because God's grand, mysterious ways
    Thy sight cannot discern.

The smallest seed which scattered falls,
    A forest may produce,
And yield a thousand precious fruits
    For God's especial use.

The tree which shelters thee from heat,
  Whose branches o'er thee wave,
Was planted by some tender hand
  Now mouldering in the grave.

Then be thou not afraid to cast
  Thy bread upon the waters,
In future years it will return
  Unto thy sons and daughters.

I THANK THEE, LORD, FOR EVERY GIFT.

I THANK thee, Lord, for every gift,
  Thy tender, loving care,
And in acknowledgment I lift
  My voice to thee in prayer.

I thank thee for the mother's love
  Which blessed my infant days,
And taught my heart to rise above,
  In songs of grateful praise.

I thank thee for the gentle wife
  Thou gavest unto me,
Who filled a long and chequered life
  With songs of harmony.

I thank thee for our children sent,
  Which, like thy faithful dove,
Have bound our hearts together with
  The olive branch of love.

I thank thee for the many friends,
   That in my darkest day,
Have shed the light of sympathy
   Upon life's weary way.

I thank thee for the troubles sent,
   The lessons they have taught,
And feel that every act of thine
   With mercy has been fraught.

And pray my heart may faithful be,
   So when my course is run,
I may not shrink, but welcome thee,
   And say, " Thy will be done."

THE WISDOM OF KING DAVID.

1 CHRONICLES, CHAPTER 21.

WHEN Satan provoked great King David
   To do what Jehovah abhorred,
His prophet proclaimed to the king,
   The anger and words of the Lord.

Thus saith the Lord — " Choose thee either
   A famine for three years to reign,
During which all the people of Israel
   Shall suffer for water and grain ;

" Or three months tormented by foes,
   Overtaken by fire and sword,
Left *alone* in thine enemies' hands,
   Unhelped by thy Master, the Lord ;

Or else God's destroying angel,
  For three days throughout all the land,
Carrying death and the pestilence with him,
  The sword of the Lord in his hand."

Then answered the king unto Gad,
  "I have sinned and am in a sad strait,
Let me fall in the hand of the Lord,
  For I know that his mercies are great.

"But let me not fall in the hand
  Of man, I beseech thee, O Lord;
I rather would trust to thy angel,
  The pestilence and the sword."

THE VICTORY OF KING ASA.

2 Chronicles, Chapter xiv.

The Ethiop came out in his pomp and pride,
  With a thousand thousand men,
And warriors in gilded chariots ride
  Through Zephathah's peaceful glen.

The tramp of his foot through the forest sounds,
  Like waves on the rock-bound coast,
And the grass lies crushed and dead on the ground,
  Trod down by the mighty host.

The vulture soars stately above the cliff,
  The jackal and beasts of prey
Creep after his track, for afar they sniff
  The feast they will have next day.

Round the watchfire's glare all the Ethiop host
    Are revelling loud and long,
And the forest echoes the conquering boast,
    The shout and the heathen song.

The moon and the quiet stars look down
    In King Zerah's silken tent,
Where his minstrel plays on his harp, to drown
    His moments in merriment.

Then again, in a camp, the pale moon steals
    One ray in a royal tent,
Where Asa, the King of Judah, kneels,
    A rev'rent suppliant bent.

And bright angels hover above the king,
    As he breathes his fervent prayer
To the God of battles, beneath his wing
    To keep him in tender care.

The prayer of King Asa is borne on high,
    To the throne of Judah's Lord,
Who frowns, and shadows across the sky,
    Envelop the Ethiop horde.

King Zerah, smitten with panic and fear,
    In darkness and gloom has fled,
And the dawn shows Asa no foe is near,
    Save the dying and the dead.

THE PRAYER OF KING ASA.
2 Chronicles, Chapter XIV.

O Lord, it is nought with thee to help
    Whether with many or few;
Thy glance can scatter the heathen host,
    As the sun melts glist'ning dew.

O Lord, in our strength we do not boast,
    But cry, help! on bended knee,
And marching against the mighty host,
    We rest, O Lord, on thee.

Thou God of *our fathers*, be the same
    To thy children in this vale,
And against us, Lord, who this day fight,
    Lord, let not man prevail.

"BE YE STRONG."
2 Chronicles, Chapter XV, Verse 7.

Be ye strong, therefore, and let not your hands
    In labor and love be weak;
In the battle of life, one who quietly stands,
    Neither glory nor profit can seek.

But ye who work patiently, ever in hope,
    By obstacles never retarded,
With fate and with fortune are fitted to cope,
    And your work will be surely rewarded.

THE PUNISHMENT OF UZZIAH.

2 CHRONICLES, CHAPTER XXVI.

In the kingdom of Judah, Uzziah was king,
On his head was the crown, on his hand was the ring,
Which the false Amaziah, his father, had worn
In his prosperous days, ere the Lord he did scorn.

In the kingdom of Judah, Uzziah was king,
And jewels and gold the Ammonites bring;
His power increased and his fame spread abroad,
Because he did right in the sight of the Lord.

As long as Uzziah, of pious accord,
Bowed not to false idols, but worshipped the Lord,
Every act of his life God did prosper and thrive,
And, vanquished before him, the heathen did drive.

He fortified towns, he made himself strong,
To punish whoever should do him a wrong;
To the kingdom of Judah he Eloth restored,
And he conquered the Arab by help of the Lord.

But when he was strong he was puffed up with pride,
He forgot it was God who had fought on his side,

And his weak heart so proudly and loftily soared,
That he thought to despise the commands of the
    Lord.

In the temple of God he dared incense to burn,
The priest of the Lord he did impiously spurn,
And before the high altar made strife and dis-
    cord,
In the holy of holies, the House of the Lord.

King Uzziah was wroth ; in his anger he dared
To resist God, who long in his mercy had spared,
When, lo ! on his forehead appeared a white spot,
Placed there by the hand of the God he forgot.

Uzziah, in sorrow, bowed low to the rod,
A leper he went from the temple of God;
His sceptre is broken, his friends all have fled,
And his throne is a stranger's, who reigns in his
    stead.

FROM DEUTERONOMY.

CHAPTER XXIV, VERSES 19, 20, 21.

WHEN thou thy harvest-field shalt reap,
    And hast forgot a sheaf,
Go not again to bear it off,
    But leave it for relief
Of some poor stranger, who in prayer,
Will recommend thee to God's care.

When thou thy olive tree shalt beat,
    Thou shalt not strike again ;

The bough that thou hast beaten once,
   Untouched it shall remain,
For some poor orphan, who in prayer,
Will recommend thee to God's care.

When in thy vineyard thou shalt pluck
   The finest of thy fruit,
Leave thou, in charity, the bunch
   Which clusters near the root,
For some poor widow, who in prayer,
Will recommend thee to God's care.

If this thou doest thou wilt show
   How thou dost love thy neighbor,
And God who doth all secrets know,
   Will bless thy work and labor,
And hearken to thy neighbor's prayer,
Which recommends thee to his care.

FROM JOB.

Chapter XXIII, Verses 3, 4.

Oh that I knew where I might find
   Jehovah's awful judgment seat,
That I might humbly plead my cause,
   And cast my burden at his feet.

I know he would not answer me,
   Or turn away in slighting scorn,
But in his mercy, strength would give,
   To one so helpless and forlorn.

I gaze, as far as eye can reach,
  Around my path, in dim despair,
But every step to me doth teach
  Some lesson of God's care ; —

That all my ways are in his hand,
  That he himself appoints my fate,
And though I fear, yet will I stand,
  And on his time and mercy wait.

"HE FEEDETH ON ASHES."

Isaiah, Chapter XLIV, v. 20.

He feeds on ashes who forgets
  The Lord the God most high,
And on some earthly idol sets
  Fond hopes which soon must die.

Bright hopes which often on our way
  Like vivid lightning flashes,
And show us by a fleeting ray,
  O man! we feed on ashes.

The pleasure of our life is vain,
  A friend may prove an adder ;
Though earthly glory we attain,
  We find it but a shadow.

The race we run and hope to win
  With others' interest clashes,
And at the end we first begin
  To find we feed on ashes.

And when upon us age shall creep,
  And dim shall grow the eye,
When over wasted time we weep,
  And sorrowing we shall sigh,

Remember there is One who yearns
  To save, — the mighty Planner,
Who in his mercy kindly turns
  Life's ashes into manna.

"TO WHOM, THEN, WILL YE LIKEN GOD?"

Isaiah, Chapter xl, v. 18.

I know not, Lord, what thou art like,
  My mind is far too base
To contemplate thy form divine,
  Or thy celestial face.

I see thee in thy mighty works,
  I feel that thou art God,
Whether to heaven I lift my eyes,
  Or bend them to the sod.

The wide-spread curtains of the dawn
  The robes of night displace,
And Nature in her loveliness,
  Reveals to me thy face;

Not only in the rising sun,
  The heavens, the earth, the sea,
But in the smallest creeping thing,
  And leaf upon the tree.

The thunder-peal, the lightning flash,
  The whirlwind and the storm,
Reveal to me that thou art near,
  In power, if not in form.

The tender blade of grass I crush,
  While thoughtless I may stand,
Shows more than superhuman skill,
  And there I see thy hand.

No space so vast thou canst not fill,
  No roof so low but there
Thy mighty spirit bows itself,
  When humbly asked in prayer.

Thy shape, O God of gods, is light,
  The light below, above,
And by that light I see and know
  Thy spirit, — God is love.

And in the thankfulness I feel
  To sing and to rejoice;
My heart says, man, thou list'nest now
  Unto thy Maker's voice.

FROM ISAIAH.

CHAPTER XL, Vs. 28, 29.

Hast thou not known, hast thou not heard
  That God the Lord Most High
Created all things by his word,
  And watches with his eye?

The waters which he measured in
  The hollow of his hand,
The mountains which he weighed in scales,
  The dwellers in his land.

He wearieth not, he fainteth not,
  His eye doth never sleep,
But, like a shepherd, tender watch
  O'er all his flock doth keep.

He giveth power unto the faint,
  Unto the weary, strength,
And when their days are almost spent,
  He adds unto their length.

That they shall soar on eagles' wings,
  Shall run and not be weary,
And on their journey never faint,
  Nor find it dark or dreary.

FROM PROVERBS.

As the bird by wandering, as the swallow by flying, so the curse causeless shall not come. — PROVERBS XXVI: 2.

The causeless curse can do no harm,
  No matter where 'tis from;
'Twill find at last its resting-place,
  From whence it first has come.

As sure as wandering bird which flies
  At daylight to the west,
Before the evening star appears,
  Returns unto her nest;

As sure as swallow, winter scared,
  Flies far to gentler clime,
As sure as he, with hurried wing,
  Returns in summer time;

So sure the causeless curse shall come
  Again unto its source,
And fill the soul which uttered it,
  With sorrow and remorse.

FROM PROVERBS.

CHAPTER XIII, V. 7.

There is a man who stints himself,
  Who sacrifices health,
Who saves each penny that he gains,
  And thinks that he has wealth.

But when upon his couch he lies,
  And Death shall by him stand,
He feels he nothing has on earth
  Except six feet of land.

And o'er the labor he has wrought,
  In sadness he doth grieve,
That in the world he nothing brought,
  And all behind must leave.

There is a man who giveth oft,
  And worldlings say is poor;
Who never turns his face away
  From suffering at his door.

Yet in his heart he riches hath,
　Which they can never know,
Who cast no sunlight on the path
　Of misery and woe.

And when Death comes to him, he'll be
　A messenger of love,
For all his riches are not here,
　But treasured up above.

FROM ISAIAH.

Chapter xxxii, v. 7.

Behold in righteousness a king
　Forever blest shall reign,
His feet shall trample time and death,
　His glory never wane.

This king shall be a hiding-place,
　From tempest and from wind,
A covert where can safely dwell
　The outcast of mankind.

As is the shadow of a rock
　In some sad, weary land,
To one who faints, so shall this king
　A rock of refuge stand.

As is the stream to one who thirsts,
　In some dry, desert place,
So shall this king a fountain be,
　Of righteousness and grace.

"IF YE HAVE FAITH AND DOUBT NOT."

St. Matthew, Chapter xxi, Vs. 21, 22.

Why should I doubt when I have heard
   The things that thou hast done?
Why should I doubt when I believe
   Thou art the Father's Son?

Why should I doubt when well I know
   Thou art *the Word* which spoke,
And o'er a dark, chaotic void
   The light from darkness broke?

Why should I doubt when earth and sea
   Were formed at thy command,
And in thine image man was made,
   The creature of thy hand?

Why should I doubt, since thou didst speak
   To Moses, on the mount?
Why should I doubt, since thou didst make
   A barren rock a fount?

Why should I doubt, Lord, when I know
   The blind were made to see,
And that the lame were made to walk,
   O Son of God, by thee?

I do not doubt, but I believe,
   That if I called on thee,
By faith a mountain I could move,
   And cast it in the sea.

I do not doubt, Lord, I believe,
  Relying on thy care,
That all I ask I shall receive,
  By trusting faith and prayer.

STEPHEN BEFORE THE COUNCIL.

Before the council Stephen stood,
  A man of faith and power,
Nor feared the haughty, steadfast gaze
  His judges on him lower.

His countenance illumined with
  The light of heavenly grace,
Shone on the darkened hall as though
  It were an angel's face.

Then spake he — "Men and brethren, hear,
  The Lord, the God most high,
Who dwelleth not in temples,
  But dwells beyond the sky.

"The God whose throne is heaven,
  Whose footstool is the earth,
Who deigned to watch o'er Moses,
  To manhood, from his birth.

"Whose hand made all these things,
  And many deeds have done,
For you who have betrayed and killed
  The holy and just One.

"For you who have received the Lord,
　　The Lord have never kept;
For you to whom he sent his Son,
　　Who for your sins has wept.

"Behold! the heavens open wide,
　　And lo! the Son doth stand;
I see him clothed in glory,
　　Beside God's strong right hand."

Then they who heard him, loudly cried,
　　With angry voice and shout,
And from the hall of judgment
　　They roughly cast him out;

And stoned him as he cried aloud,
　　"Why will ye not believe?"
And calling out, in earnest prayer,
　　"My spirit, Lord, receive."

Then kneeling down, as though to die
　　For Christ, he did rejoice;
"Lay not this sin, Lord, to their charge,"
　　He cried, with fainting voice.

And full of faith, that God the just
　　A watch o'er him would keep;
Without a murmur at their sin,
　　In Jesus fell asleep.

THE PREACHER.

The thing that has been is that which shall be,
   And that which is done shall be done:
Of all the strange things that we hear of and see,
   There is nothing new under the sun.

In wisdom I found there was mingled much grief,
   In knowledge an increase of sorrow,
For vexation of spirit I found no relief,
   And I knew not the things of to-morrow.

I communed with my heart, and in solitude said,
   What use, man, to build or to rear?
In a moment the hopes of a lifetime have fled,
   And all is but vanity here.

O heart, I will prove thee with joy and mirth,
   Therefore now enjoy thy pleasure;
I found that of laughter there soon was a dearth,
   And vanity filled up the measure.

The red wine I drained to the dregs in the chalice,
   And mingled my wisdom with folly,
My orgies and revels, in hovel or palace,
   But saddened and made melancholy.

I gathered together much silver and gold,
   And heaped up a mountain of treasure,

But where was the profit? I daily grew old,
    And labored for some stranger's pleasure.

Vanity of vanities! all life is vain,
    Though wisdom or wealth we inherit;
From all of our labor no profit we gain,
    And all is vexation of spirit.

All the days of a man are but sorrow and grief,
    And his heart hath no rest in the night;
His wealth and his wisdom can bring no relief,
    For they pass away soon from his sight.

Then I said it is better to eat and to drink,
    And enjoy the good of our labor,
And while we are living, of others to think,
    And cheerfully give to our neighbor.

As the fowl of the air, as the beast of the field,
    So man is appointed to die,
And to death all his riches and wisdom must yield,
    And his breath pass away like a sigh.

From dust all have come, both the man and the beast,
    To the dust of the earth all return,
And the worm on each carcass shall revel and feast,
    Nor the difference between them discern.

But the spirit of man soareth upward on high,
    And feels that he has a new birth,
And enraptured looks down from his home in the sky,
    To his flesh lying dead in the earth.

"REMEMBER THY CREATOR."

ECCLESIASTES, CHAPTER XII.

Remember thy Lord in the days of thy youth,
While thy heart is still pure and alive to the truth,
Ere old age shall creep on and the years shall draw nigh,
When to look back on life is to sorrow and sigh,
That thy mirth and thy joys, thy riches and treasure,
Are all in the past and afford thee no pleasure;
That the gold of thy life has been mixed with alloy,
And thy work, for a stranger *to thee* to enjoy.

In the days of thy youth, when thy hopes are all bright,
And the sun and the moon on thy path shed their light,
Ere a cloud has arisen to darken thy way,
Or a streamlet been swollen thy footsteps to stay;
Ere all thy desire for pleasure shall fail,
And thy song shall be nought but a cry and a wail;
Ere the mourners shall follow a man to his grave,
And over thy tombstone the willow shall wave.

Ere the Voice which created, His fiat has spoken,
The pitcher of life at the fountain be broken,
Ere the golden bowl break at the foot of the hill,
And the wheel at the cistern stand useless and still,
Or ever be parted the soul's silver cord,
At the touch of its Maker, Jehovah the Lord,
And the dust thou art made of return to the same,
And the spirit ascend to the God whence it came.

"BOAST NOT THYSELF OF TO-MORROW."

PROVERBS, CHAPTER XXVII, V. 1.

Boast not thyself of to-morrow,
    Thou knowest not what it may be,
Whether a day of sorrow,
    Or day of pleasure to thee.

The sun very often has set
    In a glorious golden light,
But clouds when the morning dawned,
    Have concealed him from thy sight.

To-day thy path may be strewn
    With roses on which to tread,
To-morrow sharp thorns appear,
    And the flowers lie crushed and dead.

Then boast not thyself of to-morrow,
    Live thou alone for to-day,
Pray Heaven to keep off sorrow,
    And to lead thee on thy way.

"ALL FLESH IS GRASS."

Isaiah xl.

'Mid lightning flash and thunder peal,
    Jehovah, the Most High,
Has whispered, in a spirit voice,
    Unto Isaiah — " Cry."

The prophet felt the still small voice,
    And kneeling did reply,
" O Thou, whose whisper quells the storm,
    Reveal what I shall cry."

" All flesh is grass, all flesh is grass,
    No harvest can it yield;
The glory of it all shall pass,
    Like flowers of the field.

" The grass in summer time shall droop,
    The brightest flower shall die,
Because the spirit of the Lord
    Has doomed it passing by.

" But though the grass so withereth,
    The flower so fade away,
The Word of God, the Lord of all,
    Shall stand ' till judgment day.' "

"A MAN THAT HATH FRIENDS MUST SHOW HIMSELF FRIENDLY."

PROVERBS XVIII, V. 24.

Would'st thou, O man, win many friends
  And in contentment live,
Show thou thyself a friend to be,
  And not afraid to give.

There is a Friend who closer sticks
  Than any earthly brother;
Who never fails to help the man
  That giveth to another.

Who pity hath upon the poor,
  Unto the Lord doth lend,
And by his charity will win
  Jehovah for his friend.

Jehovah, who will sevenfold
  Repay all that is given,
By happiness while living here,
  And happiness in heaven.

PRAYER OF AGUR.

Proverbs, Chap. xxx.

O God, of whom each word is pure,
    Whose every act is just,
Be thou my buckler and my shield,
    In thee I put my trust.

Remove far from me vanity,
    Lest I perchance grow proud,
And in my worldliness forget
    The tombstone and the shroud.

Give me not riches in excess,
    Lest I should grow o'erfed,
And in my pride forget to say
    Give me my daily bread.

Nor give me poverty, my God,
    Lest I too poor should feel,
And take thy holy Name in vain,
    Or in temptation steal.

But keep me in contentment, Lord,
    From every evil thing,
And let me rest in peace beneath
    The shadow of thy wing.

FATHER OF MERCIES.

Father of mercies, thy almighty will
  In heaven and earth be done ;
Thou spakest and the storm was still ;
  And stayed the fiery sun.

Long before Abraham was
  Thou wast, the great " I am,"
Jehovah, Father, Son,
  Immanuel, the Lamb.

PRAYER OF HABAKKUK.

O Lord, I have heard thy voice,
  And I trembled in my fears ;
O Lord, revive thy work
  In the midst of the fleeting years.

In wrath remember mercy,
  Spare thou thy chastening rod,
Crush me not with thy power,
  But save me by it, my God.

From the desert of Teman God came,
  From Mount Paran the Holy One ;
His glory covered the heavens,
  And his brightness was the sun.

He had horns coming out of his hands,
    Before him the wicked did cower,
In wrath he remembered mercy,
    And there was the hiding of power.

Before him the pestilence went,
    Burning coals came forth at his feet;
He stood and measured the earth,
    At his voice the wild waves retreat.

He scattered the mountains asunder,
    The perpetual hills did bow;
His ways are for everlasting,
    Before the world was as now.

Thou didst cleave the trembling earth
    With a glance of thy burning eye;
The Deep uttered loud his voice,
    And lifted his hands on high.

The sun and the moon stood still,
    At the light of thine arrows they went;
And the glittering of thy spear
    Illumined the firmament.

Thou didst march through the land in anger,
    With thy horses didst walk the wave;
Thou didst hide the might of thy power
    By punishing only to save.

At the sound of thy voice I trembled,
    My lips quivered weak with fear,
That I, in the day of trouble,
    Might call and thou not be near.

Though the fig-tree refuse to blossom,
    And no fruit shall be on the vine,
Though the flock may forsake the fold,
    Still, my Lord, I will not repine.

The Lord my God is my strength,
    To his servant he ever is kind,
He will cause me to walk in high places,
    With feet like the feet of the hind.

In the Lord I will ever rejoice,
    In the God of salvation have joy,
And praising my Lord and my God,
    My heart and my voice will employ.

PSALM IV.

Dark clouds may make the pathway night,
    And muttering thunder roll,
The lightning flash may blind the sight
    And fill with fear the soul.

But I will lay me down in peace,
    And trustfully will sleep,
For thou, Lord, wilt my fears release,
    And me in safety keep.

THE BLESSINGS OF OBEDIENCE TO GOD.

DEUTERONOMY, CHAPTER XXVIII.

If thou wilt hearken to the voice
   Of God the Lord Most High,
In all thy work thou shalt rejoice,
   And God be ever nigh.

Of blessings all these shall be thine,
   If thou by night and day
Wilt hearken to thy Maker's voice,
   And his commands obey.

The ground to thee shall yield its fruit,
   Thy cattle shall increase,
And all thy days shall blessed be,
   In plenteousness and peace.

The Lord shall riches give to thee,
   Shall rain upon thy land,
And in each season he will bless
   The labor of thy hand.

Thou health shalt have and means to lend,
   Thou shalt not need to borrow;
In pleasure every day shall end,
   And thou shalt know no sorrow.

THE ANGEL CHILD.

Mid the bustle and the strife
Of the noisy walks of life,
I pause and think, my wife,
        Of our angel child.

He came but for a day,
No longer could he stay,
Then sadly went away,
        Our angel child.

When his empty crib I see,
Where we used to bend the knee,
And pray, O God, to thee,
        For our child,

I feel the tear-drops start,
And a sorrow at my heart,
That we are far apart,
        My angel child.

But I know thou art at rest,
In the mansion of the blest,
Where children are caressed,
        My angel child.

By the God from heaven exiled,
Who in love and mercy smiled
On children undefiled,
        My angel child.

So I see thy shoes and socks,
  And thy little toy box,
And thy severed golden locks,
    My angel child.

And though bitter tears may start,
  I still my aching heart
By the calming thought, thou art
    An angel child.

THE GOODNESS OF GOD.

PSALM VIII.

When I consider all Thy works,
  And all thy wisdom scan,
I wonder thou hast done so much
  For such a worm as man.

I pause in wonder, and I ask,
  Lord, what is man to thee,
That thou to him should'st be so kind,
  Of him so mindful be?

For thou hast made him scarcely less
  Than angels round thy throne,
And, by thy hand, created him
  In image of thy own.

All beast, and fowl, and fish, to him,
  Thou gavest, Lord, for meat,
And all the great works of thy hand,
  Hast placed beneath his feet.

O Lord, our God, I wonder why,
  For man, so little worth,
That thou shouldst waste a thought on him,
  While creeping on the earth.

"THE LORD IS MY SHEPHERD."

Psalm XXIII.

The Lord is my Shepherd,
  He always is near;
With him watching over,
  I never need fear.

Beside the still waters
  He lulls me to rest,
With faith in his guidance,
  And peace in my breast.

Though I walk through the vale
  Of the shadow of death,
I have no fear of evil
  Or calumny's breath.

His rod and his staff
  My comfort shall be,
And his goodness and mercy
  Will e'er follow me.

UNTO THE LORD GIVE THANKS.

PSALM CXVIII.

Unto the Lord give thanks,
    For the Lord our God is good,
His mercy endureth forever,
    By his servant he ever hath stood.

In distress, on the Lord I called,
    And the Lord God answered me;
In high places he set me up,
    From sorrow he made me free.

If the Lord is on my side,
    I never will shrink or fear;
What can man do unto me
    When I feel that the Lord is near?

It is better to trust in the Lord,
    Than in princes or man to confide;
The Lord is my strength and my song,
    In his help I will ever abide.

This is the day he hath made,
    In it I will ever rejoice;
Who comes in the name of the Lord
    I will praise with my harp and my voice.

Save now, O Lord, I beseech,
   Prosperity send now on me,
Thou art my God and my Lord,
   I exalt and will ever praise thee.

Unto the Lord give thanks,
   For the Lord our God is good,
His mercy endureth forever,
   By his servant he ever hath stood.

UNLESS THE LORD BE WITH US.

Psalm cxxvii.

Unless the Lord be with us,
   Our labor is in vain;
Unless the Lord the city keep,
   The watch need not remain.

It is vain to rise up early,
   Or to sit up late at night,
To eat the bread of sorrow,
   Or with the world to fight;

Unless the Lord is with us
   And a watch around us keep,
For by his care he giveth,
   To his beloved, sleep.

PRAISE GOD.

Psalm CXIII.

From the rising of the sun
   To the setting of the same,
Praise ye the Lord,
   Praise his holy name.

Who is like the Lord
   Our God who dwells on high?
The heaven is his throne,
   His charriot is the sky.

He lifteth up the poor
   And the needy from the dust,
He shields all with his power,
   Who in him put their trust.

Then praise the Lord forever,
   Praise his holy name,
From the rising of the sun
   To the setting of the same.

I LOVE THE LORD MY GOD.

Psalm CXVI.

I love the Lord my God
   Because he heard my prayer,
And when I called upon him,
   Preserved me with his care.

He found me in great trouble,
　In sorrow and in grief;
I called upon his name,
　And he came to my relief.

Return unto thy rest,
　My soul, dismiss all fears,
Thy Lord has conquered death,
　And wiped away thy tears.

Unto the Lord my God
　I'll pay my daily vow,
In the presence of his people,
　Before the Lord I'll bow;

And praise his holy name
　In every land and nation,
Because he heard my voice
　In humble supplication.

"THEY THAT SOW IN TEARS."

PSALM CXXVI.

They that sow in tears,
　In joy shall reap,
Bearing precious seed,
　Going forth to weep.

Yet shall they return
　With laughter and singing,
Sorrow turned to gladness,
　Bright sheaves bringing.

"UNTO THEE, O LORD, DO I LIFT UP MY SOUL."

PSALM XXV.

Unto thee, O Lord, I lift my soul,
    To thee, the strong and just;
Hear thou, O Lord, my daily prayer,
    Thy mercy is my trust.

Show me thy ways, O Lord,
    Teach me thy narrow path;
Lead me, Lord, in thy truth,
    Judge me not in thy wrath.

Remember thy tender mercies
    To the patriarchs of old;
Remember not my transgression,
    But keep me within thy fold.

Then I can dwell at ease
    With the lowly and the meek,
And the light of thy countenance, Lord,
    Is the happiness I shall seek.

"WHO IS STRONG LIKE THE LORD?"

PSALM LXXXIX.

O Lord God of Hosts,
    Who, Lord, is strong like thee?
O Lord God of Hosts,
    Thou rulest the raging sea.

When the waves thereof arise,
  Thou stillest them with thy voice,
The heavens and earth are thine,
  In thy name they ever rejoice.

Thy throne, Lord, is justice and judgment,
  Before thee go mercy and truth;
Thou hast guarded thy humble servant
  Through all the dangers of youth.

Thou art my Father, my God!
  Thy mercy my rock of salvation;
Thy truth and thy righteousness, Lord,
  I'll praise ever, without cessation.

"THOU ART MY HIDING-PLACE, O GOD."

Psalm cxix.

Thou art my hiding-place, O God,
  My refuge and my shield;
I hope forever in thy Word,
  By my Redeemer sealed.

Thy Word, by which all things were made,
  The life, the light to see;
Thy Word made flesh, and full of grace,
  Nailed to the shameful tree.

Oh, let thy spirit, like a dove,
  Be hovering ever nigh,
To shield me while I live and move,
  To save me when I die.

"COMMIT THY WAY UNTO THE LORD."

Psalm XXXVII.

Commit thy way unto the Lord,
    The mighty and the just,
And he shall bring it soon to pass,
    If thou in him wilt trust.

Fret not thyself that others thrive,
    Nor envy any man;
God carries out his own design
    On a mysterious plan.

With faith and patience wait for him,
    And in Jehovah rest;
The end crowns all, and thou wilt find
    All things are for the best.

"HELP COMETH FROM THE LORD."

Psalm CXXI.

When clouds and shadows gather round
    The pathway which I tread,
When stirring leaf or sudden sound
    Can fill my soul with dread,
I lift my eyes, O Lord, to thee,
Who made the heaven and earth and sea.

Then like the murmuring of the wind
  On some Æolian cord,
A still, small voice speaks soft and kind,
  "Help cometh from the Lord."
That he who doth my footsteps keep,
Shall neither slumber, neither sleep.

The fiery sun throughout the day
  Shall have no power to smite;
The moon shall cast no saddening ray
  Across my path at night;
For thou my Keeper, Lord, wilt stand,
To be a shade on my right hand.

"WHOM HAVE I IN HEAVEN BUT THEE?"

PSALM LXXIII, Vs. 23, 24, 25.

In the dark and lonely night,
  My soul was filled with fear;
I called upon my God,
  And felt the Lord was near.

I felt an unseen presence
  By my bedside stand;
I felt a mighty pressure,
  Holding my right hand.

I knew the Lord had heard
  My suffering cry,
And I answered like the prophet,
  "Lord, here am I."

And like the favored Psalmist,
  I felt that I could sing
Thou wilt keep me safely, Lord,
  'Neath the shadow of thy wing.

Thou art ever by my side,
  On the sea and on the land;
Thou hast holden me, my God,
  In the dark, by my right hand.

Thou shalt guide me with thy counsel,
  And here will keep me blest,
And will afterward receive me
  To glory and to rest.

Whom have I, O my Father,
  My God in heaven, but thee?
Thou art my rock and refuge
  To which my soul would flee.

There is none upon the earth
  That I desire but thee,
My God! My strength of heart
  And portion thou shalt be.

In thee I put my trust,
  On thy promises I stand;
Thou hast always led him safely
  Thou hast holden by the hand.

THE MIGHTY POWER OF GOD.

PSALM CIV.

O LORD Jehovah, thou art great,
 In strength a mighty tower,
Surrounded on eternal thrones
 With majesty and power.

Thou coverest thyself with light
 Which beautifies the land,
And stretchest heaven's curtains wide,
 With thy light-giving hand.

The bright beams of thy chamber rest
 Upon the restless sea,
Which murmurs evermore its song,
 Great God, in praise of thee.

Thy chariot is the fleecy cloud,
 Of wild, fantastic form,
Which moves upon the wings of wind,
 The hurricane and storm.

A PRAYER — Part 1.

Psalm LXIX.

Save me, O God, for the waters come,
  Even unto my soul;
On my journey I cry in despair,
  Lest I never reach the goal.

I stand on a shattered bark,
  And I gaze towards the landing;
In the mire I sink in the dark,
  And find there is no standing.

But Thou who hearest the cry
  Of all who humbly pray,
In mercy look down, O Lord,
  And show thy servant the way.

In thee do I put my trust,
  On thy goodness, Lord, I rest,
And whatever thou willest, Lord,
  I acknowledge for the best.

THE ANSWER — Part 2.

Psalm LXXVIII.

Thou hast heard my humble cry,
  Thou hast led me safely on,
And my doubt and darkness fly
  In the morning's happy dawn.

Thou hast led me through the waters,
  To the mountain which I sought,
Where the oil of gladness flows
  From the land thy right hand bought.

O Thou who smote the rocks,
  And the waters overflowed,
O Thou that rained down manna
  For thy children, on their road,

Look thou in kindness, Lord,
  On this little piece of land,
Let it ever flow with oil,
  As the purchase of thy hand.

IN MEMORIAM.

To Brevet Brig. Gen. W. A. Thornton.

O earth, lay gently on the breast
Of Thornton, who now takes his rest,
Without a tarnish on his crest,
      A gentleman and soldier.

O flowers, quickly spring and bloom
Upon the grave and round the tomb,
Which tears will water at thy doom,
      O gentleman and soldier.

Threescore in years, yet undefiled,
In innocence a perfect child,
In duty firm yet ever mild,
      A gentleman and soldier.

Upon the earthly roll of fame
Some sudden stars may lead thy name,
And quench thy light beneath their flame,
    O gentleman and soldier.

But when we answer God's roll-call,
Before thy light their flame will pall,
And Thornton's name stand first of all,
    As Christian and as soldier.

And heavenly hosts join in the lay,
Thou hast fought well and won the day;
Henceforth with us, in glory stay,
    A saint as well as soldier.

www.ingramcontent.com/pod-product-compliance
Lightning Source LLC
Chambersburg PA
CBHW020158170426
43199CB00010B/1089